Journal Your Way To
Joy!

By Pam Farrel

3600 S. Harbor Blvd, #116
Oxnard, CA 93035
www.Love-Wise.com
© 04/2019

This journal belongs to:

_____

Joy! We all want it but creating it, cultivating it, choosing it, and holding on to it is an elusive challenge! The poet, Emily Dickenson, mused, "Find ecstasy in life; the mere sense of living is joy enough." But HOW do we find and create joy on our journey?

"Rejoice in the Lord always. I will say it again: Rejoice!" - Philippians 4:4

God placed the pursuit of joy along my life path. As a child, I discovered people who knew the Creator of joy. They greeted others with broad smiles, warm thankful hearts and kind actions. Their consistent JOY was a stark contrast to the home of my childhood which was riddled with domestic violence, unpredictable outbursts of anger, and a grey cloud of sadness and depression. I deeply desired gladness, happiness, joy and victory, so I prayed to God about my hopes and dreams for a more joyous life. God revealed that a relationship with Him, the Creator of Joy, is the key to forever unlock the gate to joy.

"No soul that seriously and constantly desires joy will ever miss it. Those who seek find. To those who knock it is opened". -- C. S. Lewis

In my midlife years, a season with an exhaustively long list of challenges and obstacles, I was reminded that joy is a choice of the heart. It is a decision of your will to embrace joy, no matter what tornado of trauma or drama hits your life. In *10 Secrets to Living Smart, Savvy and Strong*, I describe my life feeling like a beautiful hand crocheted afghan—that someone was unraveling! Nehemiah 8:10 was my lifeline, *"The Joy of the Lord is My Strength..."*

My friends were genuinely concerned for my well- being, so they would ask, "How are you doing?" I began to answer enthusiastically, "Choosin' Joy!" Well, "Choosing joy!" caught on in my friendship circle and we all gained the ability to see joy as a candle of hope glowing in the darkness. I began sharing this experience with my audiences and the results have been powerful! Waves of sadness will pummel the shores of our lives but, by "Choosing Joy!" and encouraging others do the same, there is now a tidal wave of delight growing among those willing to consistently choose joy as a lifestyle. Joy is the outgrowth and by-product of a thankful heart. An attitude of gratitude plants the seeds of celebration that will blossom into a sense of happiness, peace and serenity that most of us entitle: JOY!

"Joy, collected over time, fuels resilience." - Brene Brown

Joy also boomerangs back to us as we share the hope of internal bliss. I co-authored *Discovering Joy in Philippians: A Creative Bible Study Experience* to help others connect with the source of joy. I wanted others to discover the source of joy and the process of cultivating joy in their hearts. Much to my delight, the research for this book blessed and strengthened my own heart, life and soul.

Part of the process of keeping joy active is journaling, which helps us meditate on God's gift of gladness. I have always been a journaling enthusiast, so I started a joy journal which is now filled with a personal treasure trove that includes:

- ♥ Quotes about joy
- ♥ Favorite verses and scriptures that brought me joy or about the subject of joy
- ♥ Doodles and drawings of joy
- ♥ Notes from my Bible study on the topic of joy
- ♥ Lists of songs that brought me joy
- ♥ Moments in nature that colored joy into my world
- ♥ Memories with friends and family that caused joy to bubble up in my heart
- ♥ Snippets from comedians or humorous speakers that evoked giggles of joy
- ♥ Scientific statistics on what makes one happy or joyous

I want you to uncover your own treasure of joy producers. This journal is your sacred special place to cultivate joy, express joy, and gather up joy!

Martin Luther gave an encouraging directive: *"Go to where the joy is."*

Soon these pages will contain your personal path to JOY! ENJOY! --

Pam Farrel

choose
JOY

For the Lord has done great things for us,
and we are filled with joy.

Psalm 126:3

"God gives gifts and I give thanks and I unwrap the gift given: joy"
– Ann Voskamp

Though you have not seen him, you love him; and even though you do not see him now, you believe in him and are filled with an inexpressible and glorious joy,
(1 Peter 1:8)

"Joy is the infallible sign of the presence of God."
– Pierre Teilhard de Chardin

May the God of hope fill you with all joy and peace as you trust in him, so that you may overflow with hope by the power of the Holy Spirit. (Romans 1513)

"There is not one blade of grass, there is no color in this world that is not intended to make us rejoice."

– John Calvin

...the joy of the LORD is your strength.
(Neh 8:10)

"A joyful heart is the normal result of a heart burning with love."
– Mother Teresa

When anxiety was great within me, your consolation brought me joy.
(Psalm 94:19)

No soul that seriously and constantly desires joy
will ever miss it. Those who seek find. To those
who knock it is opened.
– C. S. Lewis

Rejoice in the Lord always. I will say it again:
Rejoice!
(Phil 4:4))

"Joy does not simply happen to us. We have to
choose joy and keep choosing it every day."
– Henri J.M. Nouwen

Be joyful in hope, patient in affliction, faithful in prayer.
(Romans 12:12)

"Scatter joy!"
– Ralph Waldo Emerson

You make known to me the path of life; you will fill me with joy in your presence,
with eternal pleasures at your right hand
.(Psalm 16:11)

The wonderful thing is that when we start spreading joy, we begin to actually experience more joy in our lives too!"
– Steve Goodier

Your statutes are my heritage forever ;they are
the joy of my heart.
(Psalm 119111)

We are called to a settled happiness in the Lord whose joy is our strength."
– Amy Carmichael

Though the fig tree does not bud and there are no grapes on the vines, though the olive crop fails and the fields produce no food, though there are no sheep in the pen and no cattle in the stalls, yet I will rejoice in the Lord, I will be joyful in God my Savior.
Habakkuk 3:17-18

The joy in your heart wasn't put there to stay. Joy isn't joy 'til you give it away
- Dolly Carlson

Rejoice with those who rejoice...
Romans 12:15

"There is joy in self-forgetfulness. So I try to make the light in others' eyes my sun, the music in others' ears my symphony, the smile on others' lips my happiness."
– Helen Keller

When anxiety was great within me, your
consolation brought me joy.
(Psalm 94:19)

Pam Farrel is an international speaker and best-selling author of more than 45 books - and would love to continue to pour joy into your life. You will find encouragement, enrichment and inspiration in her books:

For Women:

7 Simple Skills for Every Woman: Success in Keeping It All Together
Becoming a Brave New Woman: Step Into God's Plan
Woman of Influence: 10 Traits of Those Who Want to Make a Difference
Devotions for Women on the Go – coauthored with Stephen Arterburn
Discovering Hope in the Psalms: A Creative Bible Study Experience (co-authored with Jean E Jones and Karla Dornacher)

For Couples:

Men Are Like Waffles, Women Are Like Spaghetti (versions for couples, singles, teens and video curriculum great for couples or small groups)
Red Hot Monogamy- How to Keep the Spark and Sizzle in Your Love- Life
10 Best Decisions a Couple Can Make
The Secret Language of Successful Couples
A Couple's Journey with God Devotional
The First Five Years – A guide for newlyweds and those married less than 6 years
The Before You Marry Book of Questions – for couples seriously dating, engaged and wondering if marriage is the next step
52 Ways to Wow Your Husband: Put a Smile on His Face Red Hot Romance Tips for Women (and the Red Hot Wife Challenge – a 26-day journey to becoming a more loving wife)

For Parents:

10 Best Decisions Every Parent Can Make – This book captures wisdom needed from cradle to college and contains the tools and tips the Farrels used to raise their children into successful leaders

10 Questions Kids Ask About Sex- How to talk to your kids about the Birds and Bees

Got Teens? – A deep dive into the teen mind, emotions, and world with advice gathered from parents who have successfully navigated this life stage

Raising a Modern Day Princess and *Becoming a Modern Day Princess Girls' Journal* – For parents of daughters

For Singles:

10 Best Decisions a Single Can Make

Single Men Are Like Waffles, Single Women Are Like Spaghetti

For Everyone:

Pam and Bill would also love to walk alongside you and those you love through membership in Pam and Bill Farrel's Living Love-Wise Community. Simply go to www.Love-Wise.com and click on subscribe tab to select the membership plan that best suits your life and family.

Made in the USA
Monee, IL
24 April 2023